Cambridge Discovery **Interactive**

Series editor: Bob

THE PLACEBO EFFECT
THE POWER OF POSITIVE THINKING

B1+

Brian Sargent

CAMBRIDGE
UNIVERSITY PRESS

32 Avenue of the Americas, New York, NY 10013-2473, USA

Cambridge University Press is part of the University of Cambridge.

It furthers the University's mission by disseminating knowledge in the pursuit of education, learning and research at the highest international levels of excellence.

www.cambridge.org
Information on this title: www.cambridge.org/9781107622630

© Cambridge University Press 2014

This publication is in copyright. Subject to statutory exception and to the provisions of relevant collective licensing agreements, no reproduction of any part may take place without the written permission of Cambridge University Press.

First published 2014
5th printing 2016

Printed in Singapore by Markono Print Media Pte Ltd

A catalogue record for this publication is available from the British Library

Library of Congress Cataloging in Publication Data

Sargent, Brian.
  The placebo effect : the power of positive thinking : level B1+ / Brian Sargent, series editor, Bob Hastings.
     pages cm. — (Cambridge discovery interactive readers)
  ISBN 978-1-107-62263-0 (pbk. : alk. paper)
  1. Placebos (Medicine)—Juvenile literature. 2. Mind and body—Juvenile literature. I. Title.

R726.5.S27 2014
615.5—dc23

2013016510

ISBN 978-1-107-62263-0

Additional resources for this publication at www.cambridge.org

Cambridge University Press has no responsibility for the persistence or accuracy of URLs for external or third-party internet websites referred to in this publication, and does not guarantee that any content on such websites is, or will remain, accurate or appropriate.

Layout services, art direction, book design, and photo research: Q2ABillSMITH GROUP
Editorial services: Hyphen S.A.
Audio production: CityVox, New York
Video production: Q2ABillSMITH GROUP

Contents

Before You Read: Get Ready! 4

CHAPTER 1
What Is a Placebo? 6

CHAPTER 2
The Power of Suggestion 8

CHAPTER 3
Hypnosis 12

CHAPTER 4
Visualization 16

CHAPTER 5
Imagination Becomes Reality 20

CHAPTER 6
What Would You Do? 24

After You Read 26

Answer Key 28

Glossary

Before You Read: Get Ready!

Words to Know

When an action happens, sometimes it creates an effect. Match the action with its possible effect.

Action

1. The apple fell from the tree.
2. The sun went behind a cloud.
3. It began to rain heavily.

Effect

a. It was cool enough to let the children play outside all afternoon.
b. It hit me in the head and hurt me.
c. We couldn't play the big game because the field was too wet.

Words to Know

Use the words in the box to complete the paragraph.

cancer	inject	research	scan

Sarah Mathos works in a hospital. She is studying to be a doctor. During the day, she helps patients. She gives them medicine, either tablets or something to ❶ _____ under their skin. At night she reads textbooks and online articles to learn about the latest ❷ _____ into illnesses and medicines. One day, a patient with a very serious headache came into the hospital. Sarah suggested doing a brain ❸ _____ to find the problem. When the test was finished, Sarah saw that the news was not good. The patient had brain ❹ _____, a very serious disease.

Words to Know

Match the vocabulary with the correct definitions.

_____ **1** study
_____ **2** cell
_____ **3** trance

a a time in which you are not fully awake or asleep, and you are unable to control your own actions

b the smallest living part of an animal or plant

c an experiment designed to learn more about a subject

Science Words

Read the information below. You will learn more about it in this reader.

Chemistry is the study of chemicals. Chemicals are all around us and in us. Different combinations – or mixes – of chemicals control our health and behavior. For example:

- when people exercise, the brain releases chemicals called endorphins into the blood. Endorphins make you feel happy and healthy.

- when people are frightened, the brain releases the chemical adrenaline. Adrenaline gives you a burst of energy and prepares your body either to run away quickly or to fight.

? PREDICT

A doctor gives a patient a tablet, but he doesn't say what it is. He says the tablet will make the patient feel better. What do you think will happen?

5

CHAPTER 1

What Is a Placebo?

WHAT IS THE DIFFERENCE BETWEEN MEDICINE AND NO MEDICINE? SOMETIMES NOTHING AT ALL.

A **placebo** is something that has no value by itself. In medicine, a placebo is often a pill. The pill looks **identical** to medicine, but it has no real medicine in it. In the past, these pills were sometimes made of sugar. That gave placebos the name "sugar pills."

Scientists often use placebos for medical **studies**. Imagine a new medicine has been invented. The scientists want to know how well it works, so they carry out a **study**. They collect a group of people and give some of the people the new medicine. The others get a placebo. The placebo looks just like the actual medicine. The people do not know if they have gotten the real medicine or the placebo. Then, the scientists compare the two groups to see if the medicine has had any **effect**.

Because placebos are not medicine, they do not actually do anything. However, that does not mean placebos have no effect, as the story of Henry Beecher shows:

Henry Beecher was an American doctor in World War II. One day, a soldier was brought to him. The soldier had been in a battle and was hurt very badly. He needed an operation. However, Dr. Beecher had no more morphine. Morphine is a very powerful drug. It takes away a person's ability to feel pain.

Dr. Beecher did not know what to do. He was worried that without morphine, the patient would die during the operation. Finally, a nurse tried something very strange. She injected the soldier with a mix of salt and water. This mix, called a saline solution, does nothing. It is a placebo. However, the nurse told the soldier she was giving him morphine. Immediately, the soldier relaxed and said he felt very little pain. The doctor was able to operate. Dr. Beecher had just seen the "placebo effect."

EVALUATE
Why are placebos used in medical studies?

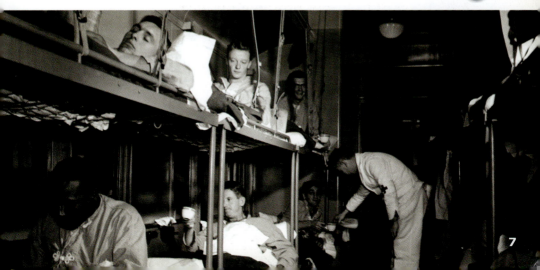

CHAPTER 2
The Power of Suggestion

DO WE BELIEVE THINGS JUST BECAUSE OTHERS TELL US THEY ARE TRUE? MAYBE MORE THAN YOU THINK.

The placebo effect has interested scientists and doctors for a very long time. It happens when a patient is given a placebo but still experiences a noticeable **positive** change. The change can happen in many different ways, but each time it is because the patient believes the placebo is really medicine. The World War II soldier experienced less pain because he thought the placebo was morphine. Placebos can also help nervous patients to relax. If a patient suffers from allergies,[1] a placebo can stop the effects of the allergy.

The placebo effect depends on the doctor's suggestion. In one study, a doctor told patients that a certain medicine would make their heart beat faster. It did. Then, the same doctor told other patients a medicine would make their heart beat slower.

[1] **allergy:** a medical condition in which something you eat, touch, or breathe has a bad effect on your body

It was also successful. In both cases, the medicine was the same placebo. The different effects were because of the effect the doctor's suggestions had on the patients' minds.

The power of suggestion works in many different ways. Sometimes the suggestion does not even need to be spoken. If, like Dr. Beecher, a doctor gives a patient a placebo instead of morphine, it is better to inject it than give it in a pill. The injected placebo is more effective. This is because an injection suggests stronger medicine is being used.

Doctors traditionally wear white lab coats.

Even a doctor's clothes have the power of suggestion. A 2005 study showed 76% of people trusted a new doctor more when he or she wore a traditional white lab coat. The lab coat suggests that the doctor has studied medicine and has experience with different illnesses.

Video Quest

False pain

Watch this video about the power of suggestion and pain. What do you think Dr. Wager hopes to learn in his study?

There have also been studies that show a doctor's white coat may have a **negative** effect. Although most people relax when speaking to a doctor, some become very nervous. This makes their blood pressure[2] rise. The doctor sees the high blood pressure and decides the person has a real health problem. This may lead to medicine for a problem that does not exist outside the doctor's office. This is known as the "white coat effect."

Interestingly, a final study on the doctor's white coat shows it even has a positive effect on the doctors themselves. A group of students was given a number of questions. Half the students were dressed normally, but the other half were given white lab coats to wear over their clothes. The group with the lab coats did much better on the test than the other group.

[2] **blood pressure:** the strength with which blood flows through your body

The researchers believe the white coats made the students feel more confident. These three studies about the white coat effect show just how powerful the power of suggestion truly is.

The power of suggestion is often used in advertising. Businesses work hard to suggest their product is better than others. A 2007 study showed how successful this can sometimes be. In it, researchers bought food from a popular American fast food restaurant. All of the food was wrapped in paper that showed the name of the restaurant. The researchers took off the restaurant's paper from half of the food and replaced it with plain[3] paper. When they gave both sets of food to a group of children, the children said that the food wrapped in the restaurant's paper tasted better than the identical food in plain paper.

[3]**plain:** simple, without colors or writing

CHAPTER 3

Hypnosis

HYPNOSIS CAN MAKE THE POWER OF SUGGESTION EVEN STRONGER.

Hypnosis is similar to the power of suggestion. Hypnosis happens when a trained person, called a hypnotist, puts another person into a trance. Many people have different opinions of what a hypnotic trance is. Some say a trance is like a time when you are neither asleep nor awake. You are in between. Others say a hypnotic trance is when you are fully awake, but you only pay attention to certain things. All agree that while you are in a trance, the hypnotist has a very strong power of suggestion over you. Researchers have been studying hypnotism for many years and have discovered interesting things about it.

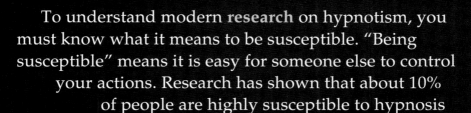

To understand modern **research** on hypnotism, you must know what it means to be susceptible. "Being susceptible" means it is easy for someone else to control your actions. Research has shown that about 10% of people are highly susceptible to hypnosis – so, easy to hypnotize. About 10% of people are not susceptible at all. The 80% of people in the middle are fairly susceptible.

In 2005, researcher Amir Raz tested hypnosis. He used a famous test called the Stroop test and a machine that takes scans of brain activity. The Stroop test is a complicated test. A person is shown the name of a color. However, the name is written in a different color. For example, the word may be "blue" but it is written in the color red. The person must say what the color of the letters is, not what the word says. So for this example, the person must say "red," because the color of the letters is red.

Red	Blue	Yellow
Brown	Pink	Black
White	Brown	Red
Red	Black	Gray
Orange	Gray	Green
Purple	White	Blue
Pink	Red	Pink

Stroop test cards

The Stroop test is difficult to do because part of the brain sees the color, but another part reads the word. This creates a disagreement, and the brain must work to decide which answer is correct. To do this, we use a part of the brain called the anterior cingulate cortex. However, Raz found that, after 25 minutes of hypnosis, highly susceptible people were able to perform better on the test. During the hypnosis, the researchers suggested that the letters of the words had no meaning. They were hoping that the hypnotic suggestion would stop the disagreement inside the brain. Brain scans showed they were successful. In the people susceptible to hypnosis, the anterior cingulate cortex showed much less activity.

Despite questions about it, hypnosis is very big business. There is hypnosis for almost everything. People use it to help them break bad habits, like smoking or biting their fingernails, or to help them do better in sports. Business people try hypnosis to help them improve their work or make more money. Artists have used hypnosis to create new and interesting kinds of art.

Hypnosis has even been used to solve crimes. In one famous case in 1978, a man had attacked and killed several women in the state of Florida. A few people saw the man, but only briefly. With a trained hypnotist, the people were able to remember more details about the man and even choose his picture out of a collection of photos. Before long, the man was caught and proven guilty of the crimes.

> **APPLY**
> Do you think hypnosis could help you in your life? What would you use it for?

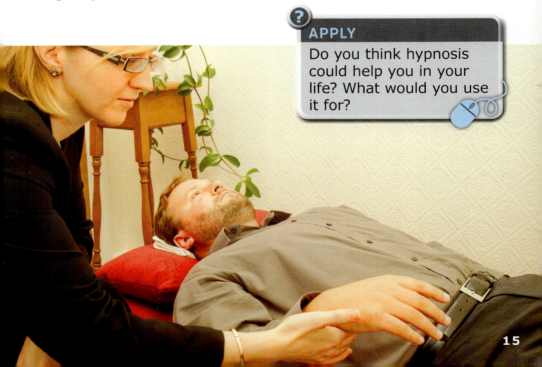

CHAPTER 4

Visualization

WILL IMAGINING GOOD HEALTH MAKE IT COME TRUE? RESEARCH SAYS SO.

A wart can be difficult to get rid of.

Can your imagination get rid of warts? Many doctors think it can. Dr. Andrew Weil of the University of Arizona tells the story of a man who had tried for years to get rid of a wart. He had even burned it off a few times, but it always grew back. Dr. Weil told him to think of a steam shovel – a large, powerful machine for digging – and to imagine it taking the wart away. The man imagined it every night, and before long, the wart was gone.

This story is not unusual. Many doctors advise their patients to use **visualization** to get rid of warts. Visualization is when you create a picture of something in your mind. Many people believe that, by picturing it in your mind, you can make it come true in your life.

Visualization is a common suggestion to help with fear. For example, some people are afraid of heights. They do not like driving on high mountain roads or looking out the windows of tall buildings. To get rid of this fear, a doctor might suggest visualization:

Visualize yourself in a high place. Fill the picture in your mind with as many details as possible. Then imagine that you are not afraid. Imagine yourself confident in this high place.

If the person does this often, the visualization becomes easy and natural. Then, when they are in a high place in real life, they remember how it felt in their visualization. The visualization is only in the mind, but people who follow these steps often suffer less fear in real life.

Many people have a fear of heights.

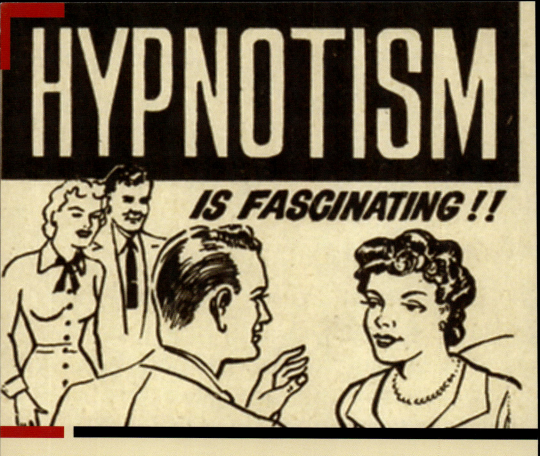

Stuttering is a speech problem in which people cannot say some sounds easily and repeat the same part of a word again and again. Stuttering usually begins in early childhood, and no one knows exactly what makes people stutter. However, visualization can help get rid of it.

It begins small, for example by imagining saying your next sentence without stuttering. Imagine forming each word and how it sounds. Then imagine giving a speech without stuttering. With success, people may be able to visualize themselves completely without a speech problem at all. After visualizing this again and again, many people who stutter find their speech improving.

Visualization is another way that the mind can control itself. Like the placebo effect, it helps what we imagine become real. However, can it control things outside the mind?

David Seidler

David Seidler is a writer who won an Oscar for the 2010 movie "The King's Speech". The movie was about a former king of England, George VI,[4] who suffered from a terrible stutter. Like the English king, Seidler stuttered during his childhood. Then, as an adult in his 60s, he got cancer of the throat.

The cancer was cured by a doctor, but it came back so Seidler tried visualization. For two weeks, he imagined himself "clean," without any cancer. Then, when he returned to the doctor, they found his cancer had disappeared. His doctor cannot explain why the cancer went away, but Seidler says it was thanks to visualization.

There are many stories like Seidler's. Some doctors believe these stories. Others do not. It will be interesting to see if any studies prove that visualization can cure cancer.

[4] **George VI:** George, the sixth

George VI, King of England, 1936-1952, with his family

CHAPTER 5

Imagination Becomes Reality

PLACEBOS ARE POWERFUL THINGS. IN SOME CASES, THEY ARE AS STRONG AS MEDICINE.

Visualization shows how what we imagine can sometimes become real. The best examples of this can certainly be found in placebos. Brain scans can show us how placebos work and how powerful their effects can be. Sometimes placebos can be as powerful as real medicines. One health problem in which placebos have worked very well is Parkinson's disease.

Cells in our brains create a chemical called dopamine, which helps control muscles.[5] In people with Parkinson's disease, the brain no longer makes enough dopamine. This means they have difficulty controlling their bodies. Often they shake and have difficulty walking or moving around.

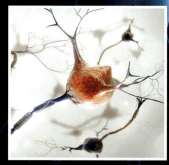

Brain cells

[5] **muscle:** a part of the body connected to bones that makes the bones move

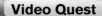

Video Quest

Imagining exercise

Watch this video about a study. What percent increase did the people who imagined exercising experience?

To help people with Parkinson's disease, scientists are developing medicines that cause the brain to make more dopamine. Parkinson's disease is interesting for placebo researchers because the amount of dopamine created by the brain can be measured by brain scans.

Parkinson's disease makes it difficult to control muscles.

In one study, a group of Parkinson's patients took a new medicine. Then, the doctors measured the amount of dopamine in the patients' brains. Next, the doctors gave the patients a placebo and told them they were getting the medicine. Again, they looked at the amount of dopamine. In many cases, there was as much dopamine created with the placebo as with the medicine. For those patients, the idea of getting the medicine was the same as actually getting the medicine.

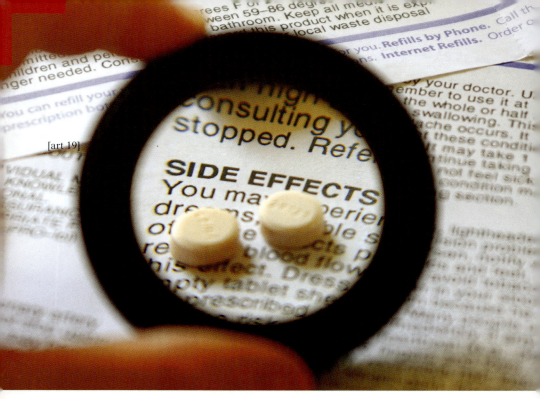

Most medicines have side effects.

The placebo effect is not always a positive effect. Lately, scientists have been very interested in the "nocebo effect." The word placebo comes from Latin. It means, "I will please" or "I will help." A nocebo is a new word created by scientists. They use it to describe a placebo that does not help. A nocebo hurts.

Most medicines have side effects. Side effects are negative effects that may happen when a person takes a medicine. For example, an allergy medicine may make you sleepy. Although placebos are not actual medicine, they also can have side effects. Dr. Richard Kradin of Massachusetts says 25% of patients taking a placebo report unpleasant side effects, often headaches.

One reason is a chemical in the brain called *CCK*.[6] CCK helps the brain feel pain. Normally, this is a good thing, because the body uses pain to keep itself safe. However, if patients are told that a side effect of a "medicine" (really a placebo) is increased pain, their brains create more CCK. As a result, the patients really do feel more pain.

Another interesting study of the "nocebo effect" was carried out in the 1960s. People were given a mixture of sugar and water and told it could make them vomit.[7] Even though it was only the doctor's suggestion, 80% of the people actually did vomit when they drank it. Whether placebos bring positive or negative effects, it is clear they work. Like hypnotism and visualization, they use the power of suggestion to create actual change.

[6] **CCK:** cholecystokinin
[7] **vomit:** bring up food or liquid from your stomach

Headaches are common side effects.

23

CHAPTER 6

What Would You Do?

A FRIEND NEEDS HELP. DO YOU THINK POSITIVE THINKING CAN CURE HIM?

Imagine you are speaking to a friend named Robert. Robert tells you some bad news: he recently learned he has cancer. Then he tells you he is planning on using visualization to get rid of the cancer.

Robert explains that, in high school, he had been a good runner, but not a great one. In races, he always won second or third place, never first. Then his coach told him to try visualization. The coach told him to imagine himself winning the races. He said to picture everything about the race, from starting off quickly to finishing first. Robert did it. Every day for a week, Robert visualized himself winning. Then, when the next race came, Robert won! The feeling was amazing!

For the rest of his high school years, Robert visualized himself winning races. It did not always work, he did not always win every race, but he won most of them.

Now Robert tells you he wants to do the same with his cancer. He wants to visualize it away. He is nervous, though. He knows cancer is more serious than a high school race. He wants to know what you think.

What do you tell Robert? What is your opinion about visualization? Do you feel it worked for him when he was in high school? Do you believe it will work for his cancer?

Robert is waiting for your answer. What is your advice?

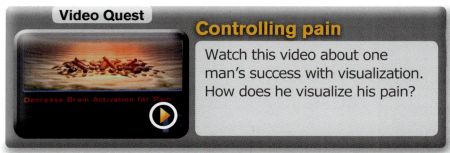

Video Quest

Controlling pain

Watch this video about one man's success with visualization. How does he visualize his pain?

After You Read

True or False

Read the sentences and choose Ⓐ (True) or Ⓑ (False).

❶ When you are in a hypnotic trance, you are asleep.
  Ⓐ True
  Ⓑ False

❷ Placebos can sometimes work as well as real medicine.
  Ⓐ True
  Ⓑ False

❸ People with Parkinson's have very little success with placebos.
  Ⓐ True
  Ⓑ False

❹ About half of all people are highly susceptible to hypnosis.
  Ⓐ True
  Ⓑ False

❺ The power of suggestion must come from a doctor or trained person.
  Ⓐ True
  Ⓑ False

Match

Choose the best match for each sentence.

_____ ❶ "Imagine yourself giving a speech with no mistakes."
_____ ❷ "You are becoming very relaxed. Become more and more relaxed."
_____ ❸ "This pill will get rid of the pain. Please take it."

ⓐ hypnosis
ⓑ the placebo effect
ⓒ visualization

Choose the Correct Answers

Read the following sentences and choose Ⓐ, Ⓑ, or Ⓒ.

1. A placebo is often used in medical studies because _____.
   - Ⓐ placebos cost less than actual medicine
   - Ⓑ researchers need to confuse patients
   - Ⓒ researchers compare placebos to actual medicine

2. Dr. Henry Beecher saw the power of the placebo when he _____.
   - Ⓐ used it to treat Parkinson's disease
   - Ⓑ used it instead of morphine
   - Ⓒ used it to get rid of warts

3. For visualization to be successful, many say you should _____.
   - Ⓐ not worry about details
   - Ⓑ picture yourself doing something you like
   - Ⓒ repeat the visualization until it feels natural

UNDERSTAND

A new medicine is invented. When scientists test it, they find a placebo has the same effect as the medicine. What does this mean about the new medicine?

Answer Key

Words to Know, page 4
1 b **2** a **3** c

Words to Know, page 4
1 inject **2** research **3** scan **4** cancer

Words to Know, page 5
1 c **2** b **3** a

Predict, page 5
Answers will vary.

Evaluate, page 7
Answers will vary.

Video Quest, page 9
Answers will vary.

Apply, page 15
Answers will vary.

Video Quest, page 21
A 28 percent increase.

Video Quest, page 25
He visualizes his pain as a campfire.

True or False, page 26
1 B **2** A **3** B **4** B **5** B

Match, page 26
1 c **2** a **3** b

Choose the Correct Answers, page 27
1 C **2** B **3** C

Understand, page 27
Answers will vary.